Russian Formalism

Russian Formalism

A Metapoetics

by PETER STEINER

Cornell University Press / Ithaca / London

First published 1984 by Cornell University Press.
Published in the United Kingdom by Cornell University Press Ltd., London.

International Standard Book Number 0-8014-1710-4
Library of Congress Catalog Card Number 84-7708

Printed in the United States of America

Librarians: Library of Congress cataloging information appears on the last page of the book.

The paper in this book is acid-free and meets the guidelines for permanence and durability of the Committee on Production Guidelines for Book Longevity of the Council on Library Resources.